STONES OF THE SKY

Las piedras del cielo

PABLO NERUDA

Stones of the Sky

TRANSLATED BY JAMES NOLAN

COPPER CANYON PRESS : PORT TOWNSEND

Translations of sections from *Stones of the Sky* have
appeared in the *Anthology of Magazine Verse and Yearbook of
American Poetry, Chiaroscuro, Green River Review, New Orleans
Review, Poetry Now, Quarry West, Stardancer,* and *Thunder
Mountain Review.*

Publication of this book was supported by a grant
from the National Endowment for the Arts.

Copper Canyon Press is in residence with Centrum
at Fort Worden State Park.

ISBN 1-55659-006-7 (cloth)
ISBN 1-55659-007-5 (paper)
Library of Congress Catalog Card Number 87-71140

Cover: Galen Garwood, monotype

COPPER CANYON PRESS
Post Office Box 271
Port Townsend
Washington 98368

TRANSLATOR'S ACKNOWLEDGMENTS

I would like to thank Susan Ballyn, Erasmo Leiva and William O'Daly for their helpful readings of this translation, which I dedicate to my *compañeros* during the months in Popayán, Kathy Gildred and Lance Martel. Lines quoted in the introduction from *Extravagaria, Art of Birds* and *Residence on Earth* are from the published translations by Alastair Reid, Jack Schmitt and Donald Walsh, respectively.

INTRODUCTION

When Pablo Neruda arrived in Paris in March of 1971 as the Chilean ambassador of the newly elected government of Salvador Allende, he carried in his suitcase fresh copies of a new book of poems, *Las piedras del cielo,* published four months earlier. Neruda would have preferred the silence and solitude of his coastal home in Isla Negra, where he had composed this latest book and spent most of 1969. Never had the public and private lives of the poet been in such contrast. His public career was mounting to a crescendo with the many national honors awarded him, his nomination to the presidency of the Republic and his vigorous campaign on behalf of his good friend Allende. Six months after his arrival in Paris, he traveled to Stockholm to receive the Nobel Prize for Literature. Yet the poet who accepted this honor was in seriously poor health, operated on twice for cancer during his final residence in Europe. This condition ultimately forced his return to Chile toward the end of 1972, less than a year before his death. During these spot-lit years, Neruda, a great public poet, was immersed in a very private, autumnal meditation on the meaning of mortality. In much of the poetry of this period, he is saying his farewells. This volume, the one carried on his reluctant mission from Isla Negra to Paris, is the work of Neruda the nature poet: a last love poem to earth.

The dramatic events toward the end of the poet's life have upstaged the important poetry he published during those years. Of the eight volumes released between 1968 and his death, only his *Call to Nixoncide and Glory to the Chilean Revolution,* sold in the streets of Santiago shortly before the military coup, seems to fit the image of the politically committed public poet we might expect to find at this time. The publication of *Extravagaria* in 1958 marked a turning inward, away from the events of the

1

world and toward a more personal voice and vision. Many of these later works are anchored in nature, and two in particular, *The Stones of Chile* (1961) and *Art of Birds* (1966), might be read as companion volumes to *Stones of the Sky*. In these three books, Neruda is a solitary observer of natural phenomena, detached, introspective, whimsically anthropomorphic, studying in great detail the living forms around him as if they alone could explain the meaning of his own life and death. As he writes in "End of the Party" (1961), in lines which are an *ars poetica* of much of the work to come, these are

> uninhabited poems, stretched between sky and autumn,
> without people, with no transportation expenses –
> for a moment I want no one in my poetry,
> I don't want to see man's signs on the blank sand,
> footprints, half-buried papers, the stigmata
> of passing. . . .

This is a Neruda alone with birds, stones, coastal promontories and the sea in his own moments of eternity at Isla Negra.

"What heaven do stones have?" Neruda asks in *Extravagaria*. Here, in *Stones of the Sky,* the poet as "man in decay" addresses crystals, precious and semi-precious stones, as well as the more modest ones, as if they could answer that question and, in the process, illuminate his own destiny. In *Stones of the Sky,* as in the earlier *The Stones of Chile,* Neruda explores his central relationship with stone both as ancestor and inheritor of his physical being. In the earlier book, the poet as a lone human seems dwarfed by the massive rock formations he describes, a private voice echoing in a public place. He closes this distance with imagination, fancying one formation a lion, another a turtle or dead sailor, as if tracing shapes in faraway clouds. In the present volume, the range of his examination is more intimate and microscopic, demonstrating a close friendship with the subtle structures of geology. This familiarity is sometimes erotic and often reciprocal: "When you touch topaz / topaz touches you." As in

the two companion volumes, many of the stones are anthropo-
morphized, treated as friends or even lovers in terms of their
mysteriously human personalities: "Turquoise, I love you / as if
you were my girlfriend, / as if you were mine." In this sense,
Stones of the Sky is much closer in format to *Art of Birds* in
assembling a gallery of personalized portraits. Yet these are more
than just affectionate nature studies. Beneath the fond details
birds reflect, as stones do, significant aspects of mortality: "Only
wings evade death . . . / if he does not fly man loses his way – /
cannot understand transparency."

Stones of the Sky brings together not only the forms and per-
spectives of its two companion volumes, but the dichotomous
meanings which Neruda attaches to stones and birds. The vision
of *Stones of the Sky* is a reconciliation between Neruda's exten-
sively elaborated oppositions of materiality and transparency, of
the immobile permanency of stone and the bird-like clarity of
spiritual flight. This is a book, as its title indicates, not about
ordinary stones but cosmic ones, those that fly: "instantly / they
grew wings / the rocks / that soared." These stones are both
solid and transparent, permanent and in constant motion. Like
birds, they follow established patterns of migration, through
endless eons of transformation. Neruda shows us

> the highway along
> which one age passed into another
> until fire or plant or liquid
> was transformed into a deep rose,
> into a spring of dense droplets,
> into the inheritance of fossils.   (VIII)

Myopic human time is the illusion. Stones are alive, Neruda
assures us as he celebrates the oceanic processes of their evolu-
tions, from opacity to clarity, from vegetable to mineral to crys-
talline forms.

The thirty sections of this poem form an extended hymn to
metamorphosis, from a molten genesis to a mineral apocalypse.

3

Neruda, the scientist, notes that "everything / is racing toward hardness" as he observes a tree which tumbles and is petrified or a cluster of yellow phenomena changed through millennia "into mellow sunlight, into pale topaz." What he calls the "damp rot" of mortal being is transformed slowly into a transcendent intelligence of geometrical structures, the "formula of fire," as darkness is converted into light, mass into energy, stones into sky. As in the poem by Gerard Manley Hopkins, "That Nature Is a Heraclitean Fire and of the Comfort of the Resurrection," Neruda enumerates the transient elements of the Heraclitean fire of natural metamorphosis, concluding with a similar faith in the ultimate reality of an "immortal diamond." Unlike Hopkins's, Neruda's mythology is based not on Christianity but on science. He captures the simple poetic essences of the complex formulae of modern geophysics by alchemically using a set of elemental symbols, all common to the Neruda cosmology and repeated in various dialectical rearrangements: stone, fire, wind, water, underground, sky, immobility, transparency, crystal and transformation. As with the devout Hopkins, the sum of Neruda's incantational equations is not a hopeless materialism but a moving interpretation of the meaning of mortality and resurrection.

Neruda demonstrates that a spiritual alchemy is also at work in the geological process, even though man's prideful individuality never quite understands "the lesson of stone." On the surface, flesh and stone seem "considerable rivals," and the agony of human mortality is expressed by the poet aware of an imminent death:

> I was rock, dark rock
> and the parting was violent,
> a gash of an alien birth:
> I want to go back
> to that sure thing,
> to home base, to the middle
> of the stone mother

> from which, I don't know how or when,
> I was torn away to be torn apart.   (XXIII)

Yet the underground of this stone mother, from which we are born and to which we return, is also where rock is crystallized and organic matter mineralized into a sky-like transparency, to be resurrected again into light. The last five sections of the poem move ritually through the stages of death, disintegration, mineralization and resurrection, culminating in a Gloria of faith in the immortality conferred by metamorphosis:

> in this point or port or birth or death
> we shall be stone, borderless night,
> unbending love, unending brilliance,
> eternal light, buried fire.   (XXX)

The lesson of stone is that man is only a tentative stage in the millennial dance of matter toward the crystalline light of the emerald or sapphire or ruby: "the only star that is ours."

In this book Neruda arrives at the alchemical wisdom of *as above, so below*, indicating how the gems buried in the earth mirror the light of the celestial bodies in a symmetry of stones and sky. The resurrection of the subterranean human star is suggested in several sections in which gems are mined from the depths of the earth, reuniting with the light from which they came:

> light's full force
> shut into the slowest of silences
> until an outburst
> resurrects the flash of its swords.   (VII)

As a central metaphor of the poem, these waiting gems are portrayed as eyes which blink open again when quarried, such as with the Chilean lapis lazuli, when "blue earth comes home to blue heaven." These eyes are also the human ones of spiritual

revelation, encrusted with mortality, which are compared to the buried crystals: "I want the light / locked inside to awaken." These eye-crystals lie under "endless earthen time" until an excavation or revelation causes them to "flash clear enough again / to see their own clarity." The eye of the mined mineral becomes the opened one of human understanding, this same "crystalline transparency" which becomes a major theme in Neruda's later work. Readers of Neruda's early poetry may be struck by the contrast between this spiritualized eye and that grotesque orb which haunts *Residence on Earth,* the "eyelid atrociously and forcibly uplifted" to take in the senseless, menacing density of the material world. This dark vision of a universe dismembered into chaotic bits becomes toward the end of Neruda's career a limpid one of unity and natural order.

There are, of course, many Nerudas: "we are many." Each major book seems to speak in the cumulative voice of the past Nerudas, as well as with a new voice. In *Stones of the Sky,* we recognize the voices of several Nerudas we already know: that of the autumnal nature poet, of Neruda the scientist, of the love poet who projects a woman's body onto geography, of the personal poet who conversationally confesses his fears and frailties. The language of the book, with its musical clarity, flowing short lines and frequent apostrophes, seems strongly related to that of the *Elemental Odes.* All of these familiar voices are integrated in order to surprise the reader with yet another Neruda, a voice of spiritual quest. Neruda was himself a translator of Blake and Whitman, and it is this voice of spiritual prophecy which resonates in *Stones of the Sky.* This Neruda is even more dominantly present in another volume published in 1970, *The Flaming Sword,* a Biblically mythic, apocalyptic parable of spiritual renewal. Neruda is still, however, primarily known in the United States as a surrealist poet associated with political protest, and in Latin America as a love poet with strong nationalist convictions. In *Stones of the Sky,* as well as in other books from this late period, we find a new Neruda, speaking with another major

voice which deserves the close attention we have given the previous ones.

I was not expecting to meet this particular Neruda at the time that I did. I first encountered this book in October of 1973, several weeks after Neruda's death, in a bookshop in Popayán, Colombia. I had been en route to the "Chile of the poets" when I learned of the horrors which had begun to unfold in that country following the coup of the previous month. This book spoke to my grief, as well as to the expansive green altitudes, the "emerald stare" of the Cauca region in which I found myself, in a country which had inspired two sections of the poem. I was living in a village outside of Popayán when I made a preliminary attempt at this translation, uncertain at first that I understood exactly what Neruda meant by "flying stones of the sky." During these months the widely studied comet Kohoutek became visible from the more mountainous areas of South America. As I watched for it, I rehearsed many of the lines from this book in my mind: "changed into a dove, / changed into a bell . . . / into a phosphorescent arrow, / into salt of the sky." I am not sure whether it was the poetry which first explained the comet, or the comet the poetry, but staring up into the South American sky they both seemed, especially at that time, an appropriate testimony to the spirit of Pablo Neruda.

JAMES NOLAN
April 1987

STONES OF THE SKY

Las piedras del cielo

I

De endurecer la tierra
se encargaron las piedras:
pronto
tuvieron alas:
las piedras
que volaron:
las que sobrevivieron
subieron
el relámpago,
dieron un grito en la noche,
un signo de agua,
una espada violeta,
un meteoro.

El cielo
suculento
no sólo tuvo nubes,
no sólo espacio con olor a oxígeno,
sino una piedra terrestre
aquí y allá, brillando,
convertida en paloma,
convertida en campana,
en magnitud, en viento
penetrante:
en fosfórica flecha, en sal del cielo.

I
_____

To harden the earth
the rocks took charge:
instantly
they grew wings:
the rocks
that soared:
the survivors
flew up
the lightning bolt,
screamed in the night,
a watermark,
a violet sword,
a meteor.

The succulent
sky
had not only clouds,
not only space smelling of oxygen,
but an earthly stone
flashing here and there
changed into a dove,
changed into a bell,
into immensity, into a piercing
wind:
        into a phosphorescent arrow,
        into salt of the sky.

El cuarzo abre los ojos en la nieve
y se cubre de espinas,
resbala en la blancura,
en su blancura:
fabrica los espejos,
se retrata en estratas y facetas:
es el erizo blanco
de las profundidades,
el hijo de la sal que sube al cielo,
el azahar helado
del silencio,
el canon de la espuma:
la transparencia que me destinaron
por virtud del orgullo de la tierra.

II

_____

Quartz opens its eyes in the snow
and grows spiky,
slipping on the white
into its own whiteness:
multiplying the mirrors
it poses in facets, at angles:
white sea urchin
from the depths,
it is son of the salt
that shoots up to heaven,
glacial orange blossom
of silence,
very principle of foam:

by virtue of the earth's pride
the clarity that awaits me.

III

Turquesa, te amo como si fueras mi novia,
como si fueras mía:
en todas partes eres:
eres recién lavada,
recién azul celeste:
recién caes del cielo:
eres los ojos del cielo:
rompes la superficie
de la tienda y del aire:
almendra azul:
uña celeste:
novia.

III

Turquoise, I love you
as if you were my girlfriend,
as if you were mine:
you are everywhere:
you are just washed,
just recently sky blue,
just fallen from above:
you are the sky's eyes:
you slice through the surface
of the shop, of the air:
blue almond:
sky talon:
bride.

IV

Cuando todo era altura,
altura,
altura,
allí esperaba la esmeralda fría,
la mirada esmeralda:
era un ojo:
miraba
y era centro del cielo,
el centro del vacío:
la esmeralda
miraba:
única, dura, inmensamente verde,
como si fuera un ojo
del océano,
ojo inmóvil del agua,
gota de Dios, victoria
del frío, torre verde.

IV

_____

When everything was high,
height,
height,
the emerald cold waited there,
the emerald stare:
  it was an eye:
  it watched
  and was the center of the sky,
  center of empty space:
  the emerald
  watched:
unique, hard, immensely green
as if it were an eye
of the ocean,
fixed stare of water,
drop of God,
victory of the cold

green tower.

V

(Es difícil decir lo que me pasó en Colombia, patria reconocida de las supremas esmeraldas. Sucede que allí buscaron una para mí, la descubrieron y la tallaron, la levantaban en los dedos todos los poetas para ofrecérmela, y, ya en lo alto de las manos de todos los poetas reunidos, mi esmeralda ascendió, piedra celestial, hasta evadirse en el aire, en medio de una tormenta que nos sacudió de miedo. En aquel país, las mariposas, especialmente las de la provincia de Muzo, brillan con fulgor indescriptible y en aquella ocasión, después de la ascensión de la esmeralda y desaparecida la tormenta, el espacio se pobló de mariposas temblorosamente azules que oscurecieron el sol envolviéndolo en un gran ramaje, como si hubiera crecido de pronto en medio de nosotros, atónitos poetas, un gran árbol azul.

Este acontecimiento sucedió en Colombia, departamento de Charaquira, en octubre de 194... Nunca recuperé la esmeralda).

V

(What happened to me in Colombia, a country well known for its exquisite emeralds, is hard to say. It came about that there they looked for one for me, they found and cut it and the fingers of all the poets lifted it up to offer me, and at the very height of the hands of all the gathered poets, my heavenly stone, my emerald ascended, slipping up into the air during a storm that shook us with fear. Now in that country the butterflies, especially the ones from the province of Muzo, shine with indescribable brilliance, and on this occasion, after the emerald's ascension and the end of the storm, the space filled with shimmering blue butterflies, eclipsing the sun and wrapping it in huge branches of leaves, as though suddenly in the midst of us, the astonished poets, there had sprouted an enormous blue tree.

This event took place in Colombia, in the province of Charaquira, in October of 194. . . . I never recovered the emerald.)

VI

Busqué una gota de agua,
de miel, de sangre: todo
se ha convertido en piedra,
en piedra pura:
lágrima o lluvia, el agua
sigue andando en la piedra:
sangre o miel caminaron
hasta el ágata.
El río despedaza
su luz líquida,
cae
el vino a la copa,
arde su suave fuego
en la copa de piedra:
el tiempo corre
como un río roto
que lleva graves muertos,
árboles despojados
de susurro, todo
corre hacia la dureza:
se irá el polvo, el otoño,
los libros y las hojas,
el agua: entonces
brillará el sol de piedra
sobre todas las piedras.

VI

I looked for a drop of water,
of honey, of blood: everything
had been turned into stone,
into sheer rock:
teardrop or raindrop, the water
kept on running into stone:
honey or blood approached
the agate.
The river churns its flowing
light to shreds: wine
falls
into the cup,
its soft flame glowing
in the stone chalice:
time runs
like a broken river
dragging the heavy dead,
trees uprooted
from their whisper, everything
is racing toward hardness:
dust and autumn,
books and trees,
water will pass away:

then a mineral sun will gleam
over all these stones.

VII

Oh actitud sumergida
en la materia,
opaco muro que resguarda
la torre de zafiro,
cáscaras de las piedras
inherentes
a la firmeza y la docilidad,
al ardiente secreto
y a la piel permanente de la noche,
ojos adentro,
adentro
del escondido resplandor,
callados
como una profecía
que un golpe claro desenterraría.
Oh claridad radiante,
naranja de la luz petrificada,
íntegra fortaleza de la luz
clausurada en lentísimo silencio
hasta que un estallido
desentierre el fulgor de sus espadas.

Oh emotion plunged
deep into substance,
dark wall that protects
the sapphire spire:
thick rinds of stones
basic to softness and strength,
to the burning secret
and the hard shell of night,
eyes inside,
inside
the encrusted radiance,
waiting quietly
as a prophecy
that a lucid stroke could unearth.
Oh dazzling transparency,
orange of petrified light,
light's full force
shut into the slowest of silences
until an outburst
resurrects the flash of its swords.

VIII

Largos labios del ágata marina,
bocas lineales, besos
transmigrados,
ríos que detuvieron sus azules
aguas de canto inmóvil.

Yo conozco
el camino
que transcurrió de una edad a una edad
hasta que fuego o vegetal o líquido
se transformaron en profunda rosa,
en manantial de gotas encerradas,
en patrimonio de la geología.

Yo duermo a veces, voy
hacia el origen, retrocedo en vilo
llevado por mi condición intrínseca
de dormilón de la naturaleza,
y en sueños extravago
despertando en el fondo de las piedras.

VIII

Long lips of marine agate,
mouths lined up, blown
kisses,
rivers that arrested their blue
waters of steady stone song.

I know
the highway along
which one age passed into another,
until fire or plant or liquid
was transformed into a deep rose,
into a spring of dense droplets,
into the inheritance of fossils.

Sometimes I sleep, I go back
to the beginning, falling back in mid-air,
wafted along by my natural state
as the sleepyhead of nature
and in dreams I drift on,
waking at the feet of great stones.

IX

Un largo día se cubrió de agua,
de fuego, de humo, de silencio, de oro,
de plata, de ceniza, de transcurso,
y allí quedó esparcido el largo día:

cayó el árbol intacto y calcinado,
un siglo y otro siglo lo cubrieron
hasta que convertido en ancha piedra
cambió de eternidad y de follaje.

IX

A lingering day was enveloped by water,
by fire, by smoke, by silence, by gold,
by silver, by ashes, by passing and there
it lay scattered, the longest of days:

the tree tumbled whole and calcified,
one century then another hid it away
until a broad slab of stone forever
replaced the rustling of its leaves.

X

Yo te invito al topacio,
a la colmena
de la piedra amarilla,
a sus abejas,
a la miel congelada
del topacio,
a su día de oro,
a la familia
de la tranquilidad reverberante:
se trata de una iglesia
mínima, establecida en una flor,
como abeja, como
la estructura del sol, hoja de otoño
de la profundidad más amarilla,
del árbol incendiado
rayo a rayo, relámpaga a corola,
insecto y miel y otoño
se transformaron en la sal del sol:
aquella miel, aquel temblor del mundo,
aquel trigo del cielo
se trabajaron hasta convertirse
en sol tranquilo, en pálido topacio.

X

I invite you to topaz,
to the beehive
of amber stone,
to its bees,
to the congealed honey
of topaz,
to its golden day,
into the domesticity
of buzzing tranquility:
it seems like a minute church
ordained on a flower
like a bee, like the sun's
anatomy, like an autumn leaf
that from the yellowest depths
of the inflamed tree
was changed, ray by ray,
lightning bolt to corolla,
with insect, honey and autumn,
into sky salt:
that honey, that world quake,
that wheatfield of sky
were tempered to turn
into mellow sunlight,

                         into pale topaz.

Del estallido a la ruptura férrea,
de la grieta al camino,
del sismo al fuego, al rodamiento, al río,
se quedó inmóvil aquel corazón
de agua celeste, de oro,
y cada veta de jaspe o sulfuro
fue un movimiento, un ala,
una gota de fuego o de rocío.

Sin mover o crecer vive la piedra?

Tiene labios el ágata marina?

No contestaré yo porque no puedo:
así fue el turbulento génesis
de las piedras ardientes y crecientes
que viven desde entonces en el frío.

XI

_____

From the explosion to the iron split,
from the crevice to the road,
from the quake to the fire,
to the turning, to the river,
that heart of sky-water, heart of gold
stayed still
and each vein of jasper or sulphur
was a rush, was a wing,
was a drop of fire or of dew.

Does the rock live without moving or growing?

Does the marine agate really have lips?

I will not answer because I cannot:
so it was, the churning genesis
of glowing and growing stones
that live on, ever since, in the cold.

XII

Yo quiero que despierte
la luz encarcelada:
flor mineral, acude
a mi conducta:

los párpados levantan la cortina
del largo tiempo espeso
hasta que aquellos ojos enterrados
vuelvan a ser y ver su transparencia.

XII

_____

I want the light
locked inside to awaken:
crystalline flower,
wake as I do:

eyelids raise the curtain
of endless earthen time
until deeply buried eyes
flash clear enough again
to see their own clarity.

XIII

———————

El liquen en la piedra, enredadera
de goma verde, enreda
el más antiguo jeroglífico,
extiende la escritura
del océano
en la roca redonda.
La lee el sol, la muerden los moluscos,
y los peces resbalan
de piedra en piedra como escalofríos.
En el silencio sigue el alfabeto
completando los signos sumergidos
en la cadera clara de la costa.

El liquen tejedor con su madeja
va y viene sube y sube
alfombrando la gruta de aire y agua
para que nadie baile sino la ola
y no suceda nada sino el viento.

XIII

The lichen on the stone, mesh
of green elastic, enmeshes
the primal hieroglyph,
stretches the scripture
of the sea
around the round rock.
The sun reads it, barnacles fade it,
and from stone to stone
the fish slither by like shivers.
Silently the alphabet goes on
spelling out its sunken syllables
along the immaculate hip of the coast.

On his loom the moss weaver
goes back and forth, higher and higher,
carpeting the caverns of air and water
so that no one dances but the wave
and nothing follows but the wind.

XIV

Piedra rodante, de agua o cordillera,
hija redonda del volcán, paloma
de la nieve,
descendiendo hacia el mar dejó la forma
su cólera perdida en los caminos,
el peñasco perdió su puntiaguda
señal mortal, entonces
como un huevo del cielo entró en el río,
siguió rodando entre las otras piedras
olvidado de su progenitura,
lejos del infernal desprendimiento.

Así, suave de cielo, llega al mar
perfecta, derrotada,
reconcentrada, insigne,
la pureza.

XIV

Rolling from lake or mountain ridge,
the stone, round volcanic
daughter, snow dove,
left its shape behind
tumbling toward the sea,
its fury spent along the way;
the boulder lost its sharp-peaked,
short-lived landmark
then like a cosmic egg
it was swept into the river where
between other stones, it kept on rolling,
its ancestor forgotten,
far from the hellish landslide.

This is how, sky-smoothed, it arrives
at the sea: perfect, worn,
renewed, renowned:
purity.

XV

Hay que recorrer la ribera
del Lago Tragosoldo en Antiñana,
temprano, cuando el rocío
tiembla en las hojas duras del canelo,
y recoger mojadas piedras, uvas
de la orilla, guijarros
encendidos, de jaspe,
piedrecitas moradas o panales
de roca, perforados
por los volcanes o las intemperies,
por el hocico del viento.

Sí, el crisolito oblongo
o el basalto etiopista
o la ciclópea carta
del granito
allí te esperan, pero nadie acude
sino el ignoto pescador hundido
en su mercadería palpitante.

Solo yo acudo, a veces,
de mañana,
a esta cita con piedras resbaladas,
mojadas, cristalinas,
cenicientas,
y con las manos llenas
de incendios apagados,

XV

You should comb over the shore
of Lake Tragosoldo in Antiñana
early, when the dew's still
trembling on the hard cinnamon leaves,
and gather up the damp stones,
lakeside grapes of jasper,
of blazing cobblestone,
little purple pebbles
or rock honeycombs bored out
by volcanoes or bad weather,
by the wind's snout.

Yes, the oblong chrysolite
or the Ethiopian basalt
or the massive map
of the granite
waits for you there, but no one comes
but the anonymous fisherman sunk
in his quivering trade.

Only I keep, sometimes
in the morning,
this appointment with slippery stones,
soaked, crystalline, ashen,
and with hands full
of burnt-out fires,

de estructuras secretas,
de almendras transparentes
regreso a mi familia,
a mis deberes,
más ignorante que cuando nací,
más simple cada día,
cada piedra.

of secret structures,
of clear almonds
I go back to my family,
to my obligations,
more ignorant than the day I was born,
more simple each day,
each stone.

XVI

Aquí está el árbol en la pura piedra,
en la evidencia, en la dura hermosura
por cien millones de años construída.
Agata y cornalina y luminaria
substituyeron savias y madera
hasta que el tronco del gigante
rechazó la mojada podredumbre
y amalgamó una estatua paralela:
el follaje viviente
se deshizo
y cuando el vertical fue derribado,
quemado el bosque, la ígnea polvareda,
la celestial ceniza lo envolvió
hasta que tiempo y lava le otorgaron
un galardón de piedra transparente.

XVI

Here as proof is the tree
in pure rock, in the sturdy beauty
forged by a hundred million years.
Agate and carnelian and sparkle
replaced sap and wood
until the giant's trunk
shed its damp rot
and a statue just like it solidified:
the living leaves
fell apart
and when its straightness was toppled,
the forest burned, an igneous dust cloud,
an astral ash wrapped it up
until time and lava awarded it
the prize of transparent stone.

XVII

Pero no alcanza la lección al hombre:
la lección de la piedra:
se desploma y deshace su materia,
su palabra y su voz se desmenuzan.

El fuego, el agua, el árbol
se endurecen,
buscan muriendo un cuerpo mineral,
hallaron el camino del fulgor:
arde la piedra en su inmovilidad
como una nueva rosa endurecida.

Cae el alma del hombre al pudridero
con su envoltura frágil y circulan
en sus venas yacentes
los besos blandos y devoradores
que consumen y habitan
el triste torreón del destruído.

No lo preserva el tiempo que lo borra:
la tierra de unos años lo aniquila:
lo disemina su espacial colegio.

La piedra limpia ignora
el pasajero paso del gusano.

XVII

But man cannot master this lesson,
the lesson of stone:
he tumbles, his body crumbles,
his word and voice unravel.

Fire, water and tree
steel themselves:
dying, they seek a mineral body
and find the road to glory:
steady, the stone shines
like a hard new rose.

With its flimsy wrapping
man's soul falls to mould
and through his sprawling veins
circle soft and ravenous kisses
that burn up and live in
the sad ruins of this tower.

Time does not mark but erases it:
in a few years the earth devours it:
schools of space strew it here and there.

The sleek stone does not know
the passing pace of the worm.

XVIII

Ilustre calcedonia,
honor del cielo,
delicada,
oval, tersa, indivisa,
resurrecta,
celebro la dulzura de tu fuego,
la dureza sincera
del homenaje en el anillo fresco
de la muchacha, no eres
el carísimo infierno del rubí,
ni la personalidad de la esmeralda.
Eres más piedra de los caminos,
sencilla como un perro,
opaca en la infinita
transmigración del agua,
cerca de la madera
de la selva olorosa,
hija de las raíces
de la tierra.

XVIII

Respectable chalcedony,
chastity of heaven,
delicate,
oval, smooth, whole,
reborn,
I sing of your fiery modesty,
the sincere hardness
of your homage in the serene ring
of the young girl: you aren't
the extravagant hell of the ruby
or the celebrity of the emerald.
You're more of a street stone,
simple as a dog,
solid in the continuous
traffic of water,
close to the wood
of the fragrant forest:
the earth's
root child.

XIX

Se concentra el silencio
en una piedra,
los círculos se cierran,
el mundo tembloroso,
guerras, pájaros, casas,
cuidades, trenes, bosques,
la ola que repite las preguntas del mar,
el sucesivo viaje de la aurora,
llega a la piedra, nuez del cielo,
testigo prodigioso.

La piedra polvorienta en un camino
conoce a Pedro y sus antecedentes,
conoce el agua desde que nació:
es la palabra muda de la tierra:
no dice nada porque es la heredera
del silencio anterior, del mar inmóvil,
de la tierra vacía.

Allí estaba la piedra antes del viento,
antes del hombre y antes de la aurora:
su primer movimiento
fue la primera música del río.

XIX

Silence is intensified
into a stone:
broken circles are closed:
the trembling world,
wars, birds, houses,
cities, trains, woods,
the wave that repeats the sea's questions,
the unending passage of dawn,
all arrive at stone, sky nut:
a substantial witness.

The dusty stone on the road
knows Pedro, and his father before,
knows the water from which he was born:
it is the mute word of earth:
it says nothing because it's the heir
of the silence before, of the motionless ocean,
of the empty land.

The stone was there before the wind,
before the man, before the dawn:
its first movement
was the first music of the river.

XX

Ronca es la americana cordillera,
nevada, hirsuta y dura,
planetaria:
allí yace el azul de los azules,
el azul soledad, azul secreto,
el nido del azul, el lapislázuli,
el azul esqueleto de mi patria.

Arde la mecha, crece el estallido
y se desgrana el pecho de la piedra:
sobre la dinamita es tierno el humo
y bajo el humo la osamenta azul,
los terrones de piedra ultramarina.

Oh catedral de azules enterrados,
sacudimiento de cristal azul,
ojo del mar cubierto por la nieve
otra vez a la luz vuelves del agua,
al día, a la piel clara
del espacio,
al cielo azul vuelve el terrestre azul.

XX

_____

Snow-peaked, shaggy and solid,
the American mountain range is harsh,
desolate as a planet:
here the blue of blues lies buried,
the blue solitude, azure secret,
the blue nursery of lapis lazuli,
the blue skeleton of my homeland.

The wick sizzles, the blast booms
and the breast of rock is threshed:
above the dynamite is a wisp of smoke
and under the smoke the blue bones,
the mounds of ultramarine stone.

Oh cathedral of catacombed blues,
jolting of blue crystal,
eye of the sea lidded with snow
blinks open again from water to light,
to day, to the clear skin
of space,
and blue earth comes home to blue heaven.

XXI

Las pétreas nubes, las amargas nubes
sobre los edificios del invierno
dejan caer los negros filamentos:
lluvia de piedra, lluvia.

La sociedad espesa
de la ciudad no sabe
que los hilos de piedra descendieron
al corazón de la ciudad de piedra.

Las nubes desembarcan saco a saco
las piedras del invierno
y cae desde arriba el agua negra,
el agua negra sobre la ciudad.

XXI

The slate clouds, the bitter clouds
let black threads dangle
over the winter buildings:
rain of stone, rain.

The dense city crowd
doesn't know that strands
of stones dropped straight
to the heart of rock city.

The clouds unload winter stones
sack by sack
and black water falls from above,
a black wash over the city.

XXII

Entré en la gruta de las amatistas:

dejé mi sangre entre espinas moradas:

cambié de piel, de vino, de criterio:

desde entonces me duelen las violetas.

XXII

I entered the amethyst grotto:

I left my blood among purple thorns:

I changed skin, wine, outlook:

ever since, violets hurt me.

XXIII

Yo soy este desnudo
mineral:
eco del subterráneo:
estoy alegre
de venir de tan lejos,
de tan tierra:
último soy, apenas
vísceras, cuerpo, manos,
que se apartaron sin saber por qué
de la roca materna,
sin esperanza de permanecer,
decidido al humano transitorio,
destinado a vivir y deshojarse.

Ah ese destino
de la perpetuidad oscurecida,
del propio ser – granito sin estatua,
materia pura, irreductible, fría:
piedra fui: piedra oscura
y fue violenta la separación,
una herida en mi ajeno nacimiento:
quiero volver
a aquella certidumbre,
al descanso central, a la matriz
de la piedra materna
de donde no sé cómo ni sé cuándo
me desprendieron para disgregarme.

XXIII

I am this naked
mineral:
echo of underneath:
I am happy
to have come so far,
from so much earth:
I am the last one, barely
guts, body, hands
that split off
from the motherlode
without knowing why,
without hope of staying,
resigned to this flighty human
fated to live and drop like a leaf.

Ah this destiny
of the darkening incessancy,
of being your own – unsculptured granite,
sheer bulk, irreducible, cold:
I was rock, dark rock
and the parting was violent,
a gash of an alien birth:
I want to go back
to that sure thing,
to home base, to the middle
of the stone mother
from which, I don't know how or when,
I was torn away to be torn apart.

XXIV

Cuando regresé de mi sétimo viaje, antes de abrir la puerta de mi casa, se me ocurrió extraviarme en el laberinto rocoso de Trasmañán, entre el peñón de Tralca y las primeras casas del Quisco Sur. En busca de una anémona de color violentísimo que muchas veces, años antes, contemplé adherida a los muros de granito que la rompiente lava con sus estallidos salados. De pronto me quedé inmovilizado frente a una antigua puerta de hierro. Creí que se trataba de un despojo del mar: no era así: empujando con fuerza cedieron los goznes y entré en una gruta de piedra amarilla que se alumbraba sola, tanta luz irradiaban grietas, estalactitas y promontorios. Sin duda alguien o algo habitó alguna vez esta morada, a juzgar por los restos de latas oxidadas que sonaron a mi paso. Llamé en voz alta por si alguien estuviera oculto entre las agujas amarillas. Extrañamente, fui respondido: era mi propia voz, pero el eco ronco se agregaba al final un lamento penetrante y agudo. Repetí la experiencia, preguntando en voz más alta aún: Hay alguien detrás de estas piedras? El eco me respondió de nuevo con mi propia voz enronquecida y luego extendió la palabra piedras con un aullido delirante, como venido de otro planeta. Un largo escalofrío me recorrió clavándome a la arena de la gruta. Apenas pude zafar los pies, lentamente, como si caminara bajo el mar, regresé hacia la puerta de hierro de la entrada. Pensaba durante el esforzado retorno que si miraba hacia atrás me convertiría en arena, en piedra dorada, en sal de estalactita. Fue toda una victoria aquella evasión silenciosa. Llegado al umbral volví la cabeza entrecerrando el ala oxidada del portón y de pronto oí de nuevo, desde el fondo de aquella oscuridad amarilla, el lamento

XXIV

When I returned from my seventh journey, even before opening the door to my house, it struck me to wander off into the rocky labyrinth of Trasmañán, in between the boulder of Tralca and the first houses of Quisco Sur. To look for a most furiously colored anemone which, on several occasions, years earlier, I observed clinging to the granite walls washed by the breakers with their salty lashes. All of a sudden, I was frozen in front of an ancient iron gate. To me it seemed like something that drifted in with the tide: but no, it wasn't: by pushing hard, the hinges creaked open and I stepped into a cavernous depth of yellow stone completely illuminated by its own incandescent crevices, stalactites and promontories. Obviously, someone or something once lived here, judging by the debris of rusted tin cans that crunched under my feet. I called out loudly to see if someone might be hidden in between the amber spires. And strangely enough, I was answered: it was my own voice, but the harsh echo was distorted by a shrill, penetrating cry. I did it again, demanding in an even louder voice: is there anyone behind these rocks? Once again, the echo responded with my own hoarsened voice, and then, with a delirious howl, the words unfurled throughout the rocks, as though coming from another planet. An intense shiver ran through me, pinning me down to the sand of the cave. I could barely free my feet, and slowly, as though walking under water, I moved back toward the gate at the entrance. I was thinking during this brave retreat that if I glanced back I would be turned into sand, or gilt rock, or into stalactite salt. A complete victory, this quiet escape. Arriving at the opening, I came to my senses pulling ajar

agudo y redoblado, como si un violín enloquecido me despidiera llorando.

Nunca me atreví a contar a nadie este suceso y desde entonces evito aquel lugar salvaje de grandes rocas marinas que castiga el océano implacable de Chile.

the rusted wing of the gate and suddenly I heard it again, twice as loud, from the very depth of the ochre darkness, the piercing wail, as though a demented violin were sending me off, weeping.

I never dared tell anyone of this incident, and ever since then I avoid that wild place of monstrous coastal rocks which torments the unforgiving ocean of Chile.

XXV

Cuando se toca el topacio
el topacio te toca:
despierta el fuego suave
como si el vino en la uva
despertara.
Aún antes de nacer, el vino claro
adentro de una piedra
busca circulación, pide palabras,
entrega su alimento misterioso,
comparte el beso de la piel humana:
el contacto sereno
de piedra y ser humano
encienden una rápida corola
que vuelve luego a ser lo que antes era:
carne y piedra: entidades enemigas.

XXV

When you touch topaz
topaz touches you:
a gentle warmth awakes
as if wine in the grape
came alive.
Even before birth, the clear wine
inside a stone
seeks routes, demands words,
hands over its mysterious food and
shares a kiss with human skin:
the smooth touch
of stone and human
inflames a quick cross-pollination
which later returns to be what it was:
flesh and stone:
          considerable rivals.

XXVI

Déjame un subterráneo, un laberinto
donde acudir después, cuando sin ojos,
sin tacto, en el vacío
quiera volver a ser o piedra muda
o mano de la sombra.

Yo sé, no puedes tú, nadie, ni nada,
otorgame este sitio, este camino,
pero, qué haré de mis pobres pasiones
si no sirvieron en la superficie
de la vida evidente
y si no busco, yo, sobrevivir,
sino sobremorir, participar
de una estación metálica y dormida,
de orígenes ardientes.

XXVI

Leave me an underground, a labyrinth
to resort to later when, without eyes,
without touch, in the emptiness,
I might want to come back to life
or to mute rock or the hand of the shadow.

I know how – not you, anyone, or anything else –
to put myself in this place, on this path
but what will I do with these pitiful desires
since they didn't work out on the outside
of the usual life,
and what if I don't seek, personally, to live on
but to die on, to be part only
of a metallic and dormant state,
of passionate beginnings.

Repártase en la crisis,
en otro génesis, en el cataclismo,
el cuerpo de la que amo,
en obsidiana, en ágata, en zafiro,
en granito azotado
por el viento de sal de Antofagasta.
Que su mínimo cuerpo,
sus pestañas,
sus pies, sus senos, sus piernas de pan,
sus anchos labios, su palabra roja
continúen la piel del alabastro:
que su corazón muerto
cante rodando y baje
con las piedras del río
hacia el océano.

XXVII

Break yourself open at the breaking point,
you, body of the one I love,
into another genesis, into the cataclysm,
into obsidian, into agate, into sapphire,
into granite whipped
by the salty wind of Antofagasta.

Let her subtle body,
her eyelashes,
her feet, her breasts, her bread loaf legs,
her full lips and lipstick word
last in the alabaster skin:

let her dead heart
sing rolling and go down,
down with the stones of the river
toward the sea.

XXVIII

El cuadrado al cristal llega cayendo
desde su simetría:
aquel que abre las puertas de la tierra
halla en la oscuridad, claro y completo,
la luz de este sistema transparente.

El cubo de la sal, los triangulares
dedos del cuarzo: el agua lineal
de los diamantes: el laberinto
del azufre y su gótico esplendor:
adentro de la nuez de la amatista
la multiplicación de los rectángulos:
todo esto hallé debajo de la tierra:
geometría enterrada:
escuela de la sal: orden del fuego.

XXVIII

The square arrives at the crystal tipping
over from its symmetry:
whoever swings open the doors of the earth
finds in the darkness, clear and complete,
the light of this lucid system.

The salt cube, the triangular
fingers of quartz: the aligned water
of diamonds: the network
of sulphur and its gothic glory:
the multiplication of rectangles
inside the kernel of amethyst:
all this I found under the earth:
buried geometry:
school of salt:
                    formula of fire.

XXIX

Hay que hablar claro de las piedras claras,
de las piedras oscuras,
de la roca ancestral, del rayo azul
que quedó prisionero en el zafiro,
del peñasco estatuario en su grandeza
irregular, del vuelo submarino,
de la esmeralda con su incendio verde.

Ahora bien, el guijarro
o la mercadería fulgurante,
el relámpago virgen del rubí
o la ola congelada de la costa
o el secreto azabache que escogió
el brillo negativo de la sombra,
pregunto yo, mortal, perecedero,
de qué madre llegaron, de qué esperma
volcánica, oceánica, fluvial,
de qué flora anterior, de cuál aroma,
interrumpido por la luz glacial?
Yo soy de aquellos hombres transitorios
que huyendo del amor en el amor
se quedaron quemados, repartidos
en carne y besos, en palabras negras
que se comió la sombra:

XXIX

We must speak clearly of the clear stones,
we must speak clearly of the dark stones,
of the ancestral rock, of the blue ray
held prisoner in the sapphire,
of the sculptured boulder in its rough
grandeur, of the wings under water,
of the emerald with its green flame.

Now, then: of the cobblestone
or of the dazzling marketplace,
the virgin flash of the ruby
or the frozen wave of the coast
or the secretive obsidian that chose
the negative glow of the shadow:
I, man in decay, ask
from what mother did they come,
from what volcanic sperm,
oceanic, overflowing,
from what flower before, from which scent
snuffed short by the glacial glare?

I am one of those vagabond men
who flying from love are in love
left burned out, broken up
into skin and kisses, into dark
words swallowed by shadow:

no soy capaz para tantos misterios:
abro los ojos y no veo nada:
toco la tierra y continúo el viaje
mientras fogata o flor, aroma o agua,
se transforman en razas de cristal,
se eternizan en obras de la luz.

I am not ready for so many mysteries:
I open my eyes and see nothing:
I touch the earth and move on,
while flame and flower, scent and water
are changed into clans of crystal,
eternalized in works of light.

XXX

Allá voy, allá voy, piedras, esperen!

Alguna vez o voz o tiempo
podemos estar juntos o ser juntos,
vivir, morir en ese gran silencio
de la dureza, madre del fulgor.

Alguna vez corriendo
por fuego de volcán o uva del río
o propaganda fiel de la frescura
o caminata inmóvil en la nieve
o polvo derribado en las provincias
de los desiertos, polvareda
de metales,
o aún más lejos, polar, patria de piedra,
zafiro helado,
antártica,
en este punto o puerto o parto o muerte
piedra seremos, noche sin banderas,
amor inmóvil, fulgor infinito,
luz de la eternidad, fuego enterrado,
orgullo condenado a su energía,
única estrella que nos pertenece.

XXX

I'm coming, I'm coming, wait up, stones!

Sometimes, some tone or season,
we are able to be together, or to be one,
to live, to die in this great hush
of hardness, mother of all glow.

Sometimes flowing
through volcano's fire or river's arbor
or fresh air's faithful circulars
or stuck trek through the snow
or caked dust in the desert
regions, metallic
dustcloud,
or even farther, the polar father of stone,
icy sapphire,
Antarctica:
in this point or port or birth or death
we shall be stone, borderless night,
unbending love, unending brilliance,
eternal light, buried fire,
pride condemned to its intensity:

the only star that is ours.

ABOUT THE TRANSLATOR

James Nolan's translations of Neruda and other Spanish language poets have appeared widely in various magazines. The two collections of his own poetry are *Why I Live in the Forest* and *What Moves Is Not the Wind*, both published by Wesleyan University Press. The recipient of National Endowment for the Arts and Fulbright Lectureship grants, he has taught literature and writing at universities in Barcelona, Beijing, Florida, and San Francisco.

The type in this book is Sabon.

Composition by Fjord Press Typography.

Book design by Tree Swenson.